Jo Evans grew up in a family where emotions and feelings were rarely discussed or acknowledged. At the age of 5 she was sent to Dulwich College Preparatory School, where the headmaster became a family friend. Five years later, that same headmaster betrayed the trust placed in him by Jo and her family when he began systematically abusing 10-year-old Jo and, it later transpired, many of her classmates. The after-effects of this traumatic time remained with Jo into her adult life, and eventually she summoned up the courage to bring her abuser to court, and a change in the law on plea bargaining came about as a direct result of that bravery.

Jo Evans was born in Kent in 1965, the youngest of four children. After leaving school Jo worked in London as a nanny and went to America to work in a children's summer camp, before marrying and settling in West Sussex. She is now a school governor and full-time mother of three children of her own.

AN INVISIBLE CHILD

Jo Evans

The Book Guild Ltd
Sussex, England

First published in Great Britain in 2003 by
The Book Guild Ltd
25 High Street
Lewes, East Sussex
BN7 2LU

Typesetting in Garamond by
SetSystems Ltd, Saffron Walden, Essex

Printed in Great Britain by
CPI Bath

A catalogue record for this book is
available from the British Library

ISBN 1 85776 893 0

This book is dedicated to the memory
of my sister, Hilary Williams

Acknowledgements

To my husband Stuart – thank you for opening the door and for not walking away when you would have been quite justified. Your support meant more than I can say. I love you.

To my beautiful, wonderful children – be happy, be strong and be everything you want to be in this life. I love you.

To my friends – Pat, Debbie, Angie and all of you who know who you are. I could not have done this without you, thank you for the hugs and the comfort, but most of all, thank you for just listening to me.

To my sister Karen – thank God for five-year diaries! I love you very much.

To the 'Group of 8' – this book is for all of you and all those out there who will recognize themselves in our experiences.

To Sarah Harman – thank you for your professionalism, dedication and patience.

And finally, to my darling sister Hilly. Words cannot express how much I miss you. You were my one ally as a child and then we lost you, but I have felt your footsteps beside me every single day and you have given me so much strength. This fight was for you as much as me. Jo xx

My Story Begins

September mornings are, to me, nature's masterpiece. The misty start to a crisp autumn day has always filled me with awe at the earth's ability to change its overcoat with each new season, covering the neatly cut lawns with a Persian rug made of every leaf imaginable of gold and copper red. My children squeal with delight at the sight of their own breath and there is something comforting about wrapping up warm to face the morning journey to school. But for me, September has not always brought such delight and anticipation. September when I was a child could mean only one thing – it was time for a new term and my freedom of the summer was at an end. It was time for me to become invisible.

I was born Joanna Helen Williams on June 17th 1965 at home, my delivery being so quick that my father didn't make it to my mother's side in time. He arrived to find me already in my crib, being poked and prodded by my three elder siblings. I was born into a normal, middle-class family; my father was a respected consultant and my mother worked as a physiotherapist in our village Cottage Hospital. My siblings and I were fortunate that my parents could give us a comfortable life, and we lived in a spacious home in the village of Hawkhurst in Kent. I don't recall my father being home very much, he worked long hours and was often on duty late into the evening. My mother was very much the main parent in our home and I remember being slightly frightened of my father. It was to him that the main discipline fell and very often the threat of his wrath would be enough to keep the four of us from overstepping the mark and misbehaving. This fear was probably totally misplaced as I don't have any memories of severe punishment from my father but he was often very tired and would come home irritable, my mother would tell us not to bother him which created this aloof person to whom we felt unable to connect. It seems very sad to me now that by trying to work hard and provide for us, he put emotional distance between us that we seem to have been unable to breach, even after all these years. There were foreign holidays every summer and as children we never went without food or warmth, but emotionally we were never a particularly close family. My father had had a difficult upbringing himself with a stern, disciplinarian father and subsequently found communicating with his children on an emotional level almost impossible. Open displays of affection were rare and I don't recall ever hearing my parents say 'I love you' to us or even each other. We were therefore uncomfortable with any physical contact with other people as we had never experienced it on any level. How I used to envy the openness of other families and their total lack of embarrassment at declaring their feelings for each other, it seemed to me that they were crude and I probably judged them for being so.

My mother's upbringing couldn't have been more different from my father's, she was raised overseas in an era that encouraged servants and maids and although materialistically she would have been considered fortunate, she too was never taught the value of displaying emotions. She was sent away to boarding school and was taught to keep smiling and just make the best of each situation. A 'stiff upper lip' was how she dealt with being separated from her mother, indeed she didn't see either of her parents for over two years whilst she was at school in England, an inconceivable notion nowadays but not unusual during the war. Two parents from totally different backgrounds but united in not understanding emotions or how to deal with them, the result being that they couldn't show us that they did love us.

Hawkhurst was a large village, but we went to school ten miles away, which meant that as children we didn't have many local friends. We only ever really spent time with each other, and we would disappear for hours on end riding our bikes around the numerous country lanes, or walking our family dog Meg through the fields that surrounded our home. It was an idyllic scenario and as a result we were able to create our own way of life, detached from the tension that so often surrounded us when the whole family was together. My parents' social circle was also widespread, mainly colleagues of my father's and a handful of my mother's women friends, but mainly influential people, high achievers who shared the same family values. We were encouraged to become friends with their children and I recall many occasions of unbearable awkwardness trying to find things to say. It is very hard to have your friends chosen for you because inevitably you find that in actual fact, you have nothing in common and they don't really want to play with you either. But we were expected to entertain them whilst our respective parents socialized with each other so we did the best we could. The main common factor between all our families was the desire to send all of us to a private school in the nearest big town, Cranbrook. And so, in 1970 at the tender age of 5, I followed my three elder siblings to Dulwich College Preparatory School and began a process that eventually shaped the next 25 years of my life.

The school was split into three separate communities. There was Nash House into whom all 5-year-olds went for about 2 years and then we would move down the driveway to Little Stream, an all-girls section of the school. The boys would move up the driveway to Coursehorn and we would remain segregated until the age of 10 when our final two years would become mixed. 'Little Stream' had its own headmistress and it wasn't until the girls moved up to Coursehorn that we had any contact with the school's overall headmaster who was ultimately in charge of all three communities. Academically, the school was used to creating high achievers in their pupils and indeed my two sisters and elder brother had all flourished, I would describe myself as a 'plodder', doing enough to stay out of trouble but not particularly brilliant. Unfortunately I was constantly reminded at school, and indeed at home, of the difference between myself and the other three, it seems that people were under the impression that if they made comparisons to me then it would make me work harder and achieve more, an opinion that ultimately backfired as it made me defiant and resentful. If you are told enough times that you are unintelligent then you eventually begin to give up trying to prove otherwise. To this day with my own children, however small the achievement, they are always praised and encouraged and there is no such word as failure. Each child must be allowed to be their own person and they will become what they choose to become, putting them down is never an option and something that I would never do. I know I was only young but I still remember feeling inadequate and believing that I truly must be stupid if all these people were telling me so.

Sometime in the early 1970s my parents developed a close friendship with the headmaster and his family, how it came about I don't know but it did and suddenly we were holidaying together and spending weekends and Christmas in each others' company. There is something unnerving for any child to have to spend time with their teachers away from school, there is always the fear that school work will be discussed and perhaps 'tales told' on you. I found it especially uncomfortable due to my obvious lack of academic interest and would try and take a back seat around the table during the regular meals we shared. This family consisted of two children of similar age to my elder sisters and I do remember happy times playing together. Both sets of parents seemed to care about each others' children, the situation developed into one of trust and we became an extension of each others' families. Ideal, in theory.

Early in 1975 my mother's sister died tragically whilst living abroad. Myself and my siblings were sent to stay with our headmaster at their house within the school grounds whilst my parents were away and it was during this stay that I realized that the boundaries of my relation-ship with this man were not as clear as perhaps I had thought. Rather than being the father figure I had begun to see him as, an incident involving bathtime caused me anxiety and confusion as to what was normal and what was not. I had requested to be able to take a bath and was obviously told that I could do so. I had filled the bath with water and was just about to get in, when my headmaster walked right into the bathroom without knocking and told me that he had 'come to see if I needed any help'. I was mortified and embarrassed and remember trying to grab a towel. I told him that I was fine and waited for him to leave. He stood there for what seemed like an eternity, unashamedly looking at me and eventually smiled and sauntered out. When I then tried to lock the door I discovered that there was no lock. Faced with the possible humiliation of having him walk in again while I was in the bath, I sat on the floor for an acceptable period of time and then pulled out the plug to make him think I had finished. From that day, until we went home, I never tried to take a bath whilst he was in the house, or I would wait until one of my sisters was around and ask them to sit with me, although I never told them why. This incident left me feeling uneasy, I was only 10 years old but something inside me told me that to walk in on someone in the bathroom wasn't right, but then again, he was my father's closest friend and why would he deliberately want to embarrass me? I tried to put it out of my head and of course, I never told my parents.

Not telling my parents became the number one rule in my life pretty much from that day onwards. I had unconsciously become a pawn in another person's game of life, and walking into the bathroom was nothing compared to what was to follow. Unbeknown to me, I became another statistic in his game of control.

Secrets and Lies

I don't recall the exact date when my abuse at the hands of this man began, I just know that all that my life had been before ended suddenly and without warning with a simple command 'please go to the headmaster's study'. The explanation was typical, my work wasn't up to scratch and the headmaster wished to speak to me about possible extra tuition.

The study in the main house was a forbidding and formal place. I remember still the smell of the leather from the chairs, and the highly polished mahogany table that dominated this enormous room. He was seated at the end of the table with my books laid out in front of him and I was ordered to sit next to him on another chair – he then embarked on 20 minutes of rebuking me for the standard of my work, along with the occasional comment on how disappointed my parents would be if I failed to meet the necessary grade to move up to senior school. I remember not speaking or being asked to speak throughout his address to me, the fear of reprisal from home was such an effective weapon that it must have become apparent to him from this moment on that I was unlikely to put up resistance to what was to come. This knowledge to a man of his power was the basis on which all future 'sessions' would be built. At some point after the lecture, I found myself being pulled from my chair and quickly and fairly violently being laid across his lap. It all happened so fast that I was staring at the legs of chair and his shoes before I really knew what was happening. He then removed my outer clothing by pulling my school dress up to my neck and proceeded to pull my underwear down to my ankles. I shall never forget the feeling of being totally vulnerable and exposed, but above all I remember the fear. What would he do next? My answer came when he began to rub his hands over my lower torso in a rhythmic motion, and all the while he was telling me how bad I was and how if I didn't improve then he would have no option but to inform my family. The rubbing became faster and harder until suddenly I was wrenched onto my feet and instructed to leave his study, he would say nothing else. The impact of what had happened hit me full force when I left his study, my legs were shaking and I felt physically sick. I could not understand why he would subject me to such treatment and although I was young, mentally and physically, I knew in my heart that he had been wrong. But I also knew in my heart that it would be impossible for me to tell anyone what had happened because I could not risk him carrying out his threats to me. I was caught, I knew it – and I know that he did too.

That evening, sitting alone in my bedroom on the pretence of doing homework, my mind went over and over what had happened to me that day. I can honestly say that never since then have I ever felt such fear or trepidation. I wondered what I had done wrong to make him punish me in such a way, for punishment was surely the motive for his actions? I decided that he must have sought permission from my father to discipline me and therefore must have been allowed to do so, in which case there were no circumstances at home that would prompt me to mention it to anyone. My only resolve would be to keep out of trouble and stop being naughty. But in my heart I knew that I hadn't actually done anything bad. I racked my brains to try and think of any incidents during class that I might have forgotten that would warrant punishment from the headmaster, but could find none. I had never been a disruptive child, I had always been taught to have the utmost respect for my elders, especially my teachers, and wouldn't dream of speaking out of turn or being rude to them, indeed I was probably ridiculed by my classmates for being a 'goody two-shoes'. If there *was* a reason for my punishment, I couldn't find it.

From that day my visits to his study became a regular occurrence. He would seek me out in my classroom, in the gym hall and even in the playground, telling my teachers that he needed to give me extra maths, extra English or just some made up excuse. He was the headteacher and therefore none of his staff would ever have questioned his request for a pupil, and I knew that during school hours there would be no escape. He became the demon that controlled me. I remember the fear of the clock on the wall of our kitchen at home, when the hands reached a certain point it would be time for me to leave the safety of my bedroom and embark on another day of trying to become invisible. I tried many ways to escape. School corridors would harbour secret alcoves that only I knew of and it would be there that I would run to when I heard the familiar shuffle of the man with the soft grey slip-on shoes. If I sat at the back of the class I could pretend no-one could hear or see me and if I stayed very still, perhaps they would forget I existed at all and would have no reason to send me for punishment, the only problem being that a child in fear loses the ability to concentrate. And a child who can't concentrate loses the ability to study and a child who can't study is sent to the 'headmaster's room'. My abiding memory of that time is of feeling great sadness and constant fear. There were times that I wished I could be brave enough to take one of the bottles from my parents' medicine cupboard and slip away into the fields and take myself to find peace, but I knew I never would. I knew that I must be a coward – for not telling anybody about my abuse and for not being able to take my own life. I was only 11 years old but I already hated myself for what I had become.

My body was violated in the same way every time and I came to know the routine, and because of this knowledge I became accustomed to switching off whilst it was happening. I remember making myself go to a 'happy place' even though the tears would be streaming down my face. No words were ever spoken by my abuser whilst I was exposed and vulnerable and the silence of that room remains vivid. At the age I was then, the silence was more frightening than being reprimanded because if my headmaster wasn't abusing me verbally then it could only mean that he was about to abuse me physically. How I longed to just be shouted at, sworn out, given extra homework, anything but being stripped naked day after day. Clothing at least gives you something to hide behind, remove the outer shell completely and you feel that even your soul has been exposed.

One thing that I do believe is that every child has the fundamental right to make the transition into adulthood with support, love and understanding. Puberty has to be the most difficult time of all our lives when it comes to accepting who you are and what you are about to become, and this transition shapes us as adults. The way we feel about our bodies is vital to how we handle ourselves within relationships of every kind, whether it be as someone's partner, someone's child or someone's parent. If you interfere with nature then the damage is untold.

I entered puberty at 12 years old. I hated it, not because I wanted to resist growing up but because the abuse continued as before, regardless of which week of the month it was. To this day, the humiliation of being naked from the waist down at the time of my period remains with me. The knowledge that another person felt it unnecessary to show me the most basic form of respect for my privacy has left my self-esteem and the way I feel about my body terribly damaged. He would sometimes laugh whilst he was abusing me, as if he deliberately wanted to humiliate me further, and he was oblivious to my obvious distress and my feeble attempts to pull my underwear back up. It must have been so obvious that I was desperately trying to maintain an element of dignity and yet it seemed to excite him all the more. These terrible sessions instilled in me my life-long hatred of my body and its natural cycles, and I have spent my adult life covering every part of me with layers of clothing in a desperate attempt to ward off unwanted looks of any kind. During my three pregnancies I have always refused to be examined, even though I would be reprimanded by the doctors for putting my babies at risk by not allowing basic checks on me. I could not face having to remove my clothing and allowing a stranger access to my body. As an adult I knew that I could say 'no' and so I did, even at the risk to my babies. In March 2001, I finally got what I had waited for all of my adult life. I requested, and was granted, a full hysterectomy, thereby putting an end to monthly cycles forever. I have never felt so liberated in my entire life, despite having major surgery and a long period of recovery I was finally rid of the memories of being naked during a period and I will never have to feel so dirty again.

Outside of school the change in me was only to be expected. I became withdrawn and frightened of my own shadow. I spent hours in my bedroom listening to music, trying to lose myself in the lyrics and imagine I was living a life away from reality in exotic places with no men in authority. I felt isolated from the rest of my family, I assume because I felt different from them. Having a family that never discussed anything of a personal or intimate nature, there was never going to be a conversation about my abuse, and in fact if the change in me was noticed, my parents never commented or asked about it, so my wall of silence remained. I trusted no one and didn't have the confidence to speak to people. Some of my girlfriends had the most wonderful fathers but I couldn't bear to be near them. In my young head, any man was a threat and at any time one of them could call upon me in the way that my headmaster did.

Being close family friends of my parents, my abuser and his family were frequent visitors to our home. I recall the sly smirk on his face when he greeted me and the way he would make a point of kissing me hello and goodbye with too much familiarity that only I noticed. I was never abused during these visits but it meant that he had infil-trated my private home life. Even school holidays were spent abroad with them, and although on these occasions I was physically out of bounds to him, the psychological hold he had over me would cast a black cloud over my precious time away from school and it seemed that I would never ever be free.

In the summer of 1978 I was finally old enough to leave the school and head for senior school. There is no description adequate to describe the feelings when I awoke for my very last day in hell. For 18 months I had been abused almost daily and, at last, it would be over. I might, as if by magic, turn into a normal 12-year-old like my peers. For the first time in all those months I went to school that day with a skip in my step. My delight and anticipation, however, were short-lived. As if wanting to prolong my pain, I was once again called to the study and once again subjected to what proved to be the final but longest session of abuse. He seemed determined to leave me with a lasting memory and I felt he was angry that after that day I would no longer be available to him. For the first time I actually left his study sobbing; before I had always composed myself before facing my classmates and teachers again but this time it was too much to bear. Possibly it was the relief of leaving his study for the last time, possibly it was frustration at being abused on my very last day, perhaps I had hoped that if he had any decency he would have left me alone to enjoy the excitement that goes with the final day of term.

As I left his study for the last time, I came face to face with one of my oldest friends who asked me what was the matter. I proceeded for the very first time in nearly two years to finally tell someone what had been happening to me.

Darkening Skies

Absolute terror is the first recollection I have of telling my friend what had happened. I had been threatened so many times about the consequences and was so angry with myself for being so weak as to tell someone. I begged my friend not to tell her mother who was a close friend of my own, I was terrified of what would happen if she did, and she dutifully promised that she would remain silent. Thankfully, although at the time it didn't feel that way, she did not keep her promise. She did tell her mother, and a few hours later when I was at home the telephone rang and her mother asked to speak to me. Of all the conversations I have had in my life, I recall this one as being the most difficult. My own mother and I had never spoken about intimate physical things and yet this lady on the end of the phone was asking me to tell her what had happened. The main memory I have is of the compassion in her voice and the obvious concern for me, as she told me that I must tell my mother. Through the gentle persuasion she gave me the strength and courage to open up to my mother.

You would expect that this conversation would mean the end of all the pain. Alas, it was not. Even at the point of revealing what had happened I realized that I could not tell my mother the truth. I didn't know her well enough to be that intimate and above all else, I knew that this time next week we might be sitting down to another Sunday lunch with my abuser and his family. So I told her he had touched me through my clothing on a couple of occasions and that I had felt uncomfortable and wanted him to stop but he didn't. Her reaction was as you would expect, horror, tears and desperate to know the details, details that I couldn't and didn't tell her. I was embarrassed and all I wanted to do was escape to the sanctuary of my bedroom and forget all about it. My nightmare would be that she would tell my father and the thought of him knowing anything intimate about me was more than I could face. Of course she did tell him and they both came to my room and sat on my bed and cried, and I wanted the earth to open up and swallow me. The word 'humiliated' doesn't seem strong enough to describe how I felt, but all I knew was that I wanted to be left alone to pretend it had never happened.

In the days and weeks that followed, our conversation was never referred to again. I had absolutely no idea what, if any, action they had taken and would only find out nearly 25 years later that my father had been to see this man, but no serious action was ever taken and his argument of just punishing me was accepted. All I knew then was that I had told about my abuse and yet nothing changed within our family. My siblings never mentioned it, so I assumed that they didn't know, and it was only years later that they told me that in fact they did know, but our parents had instructed them never to talk about it. This discovery hurt me enormously, I was always close to my siblings and had desperately wanted to turn to them for support but when they hadn't mentioned my abuse I had assumed that they didn't care. To find out otherwise so many years later made me so upset. I could have unburdened so many of my thoughts and feelings and perhaps this would have enabled me to move forward, but alas it was not to be.

The final insult came only a matter of weeks later when the visiting between our two families began again and I was expected to be in the company of the man who I had told my parents had abused me for nearly two years. The message to me as a 12-year-old was, 'it can't have been that bad and we're sure you misunderstood the fact that he was punishing you'. I felt so insignificant. Their friendship with this family was obviously more important than my suffering and it was at that point that I knew it was a subject about which I could never speak to my parents again. Just a few months later my parents were asked to be godparents to my abuser's newly born child, and my parents agreed. What more could I do? Their priorities were obvious.

A Lonely Child

The September after leaving Dulwich College, I began a new school term at Cranbrook School. Although relieved at what I hoped would be a fresh start for me, I was also anxious, knowing that the teaching staff at my new school would be predominantly male. Life at my new school was difficult. Removed from the threat of abuse I was obviously happier but I had developed a total mistrust of males in authority, which became a problem, as almost all of my teachers were male. I was convinced that at any time, one of them would pick up where my former headmaster had left off and the nightmare would begin again. Subsequently I did not do well academically and threw myself into sport, which for the girls was supervised by a female PE teacher. I excelled at hockey, played for the school netball team and also played tennis for the school. Sport was my way of finally enjoying school life and I cared nothing for exams or books. The restrictions of the classroom reminded me too much of the enclosures of the study I had left behind. I needed to be free from constraint and I found that freedom on the playing fields and the tennis courts. Days of bad weather meant frustration at being kept indoors and I longed for lessons to be over so I could escape.

Although many of my peers from my previous school had joined me at Cranbrook, I did not make many new friends. I was desperately shy and mistrustful of people I didn't know. Boyfriends were few and far between and even the ones I went out with were never more than acqaintances. This sounds strange to me now but if any boy asked me out, I always felt that I had to say 'yes' – because I wasn't allowed to say 'no'. Freedom of choice regarding me personally had never been permitted before, as my abuser had always made the decisions regarding my body, and I carried this thought process with me. How I envied my high-spirited friends who had devoted boyfriends, they always seemed to be having so much fun being part of a couple, but being part of a couple wasn't really what I ever wanted to be. Keeping myself alone meant that I could keep myself safe and that was my way of surviving. So I stayed the wallflower at the school discos, avoiding eye contact with the boys in case one of them asked me to dance and breathing a sigh of relief when they passed me by. And all this time, home life continued much as before. Any closeness that might have existed before my abuse was rejected by me – we were a family of six but in reality there were five people and one outsider. Through choice I retreated into a world that only I could control and because of this I survived, I became my own family and my own best friend, it was much safer that way.

In 1980 I took my O levels and didn't do well at all. I was expecting it but my family showed their disappointment – unfortunately for me my three elder siblings had gone on to great achievements, indeed my elder sister had become Head Girl in her final year at Cranbrook and my results let the family down. My father insisted I stay on and re-take two of the exams, which I did and eventually in 1981 I was allowed to leave the education system behind me, I left the school with five O levels and joy in my heart.

I had never really thought about what I wanted to do with my life, I imagine I had been too busy just trying to get through each school day, so for the next few weeks I listened to my parents discussing what I should do next. If I'm honest, it never really occurred to me to speak out because lack of self-confidence made me think that I wasn't capable of making those kind of decisions anyway. I would make the wrong choice so I might as well leave it up to the family to decide my future. The woman I have become now finds it incredible that I would have allowed such a thing to happen, but I have to remember the child that I was then and accept that we are two very, very different people. Anyway, the decision was made that I would have a year off and then I would attend secretarial college with a view to becoming a secretary. So my mother and I bought *The Lady* magazine and answered an advert to be a 'mother's help' in London. We went for an interview and I subsequently got the job. I left home one Sunday morning and on the Monday found myself living away from home for the first time, in someone else's house, being expected to look after two children under the age of 3. I had absolutely no idea how it even happened. I knew that I wanted to be away from my family, I also knew that I quite liked the idea of looking after children, but I was only 16 years old and had never even changed a nappy, let alone managed my own finances or even cooked a meal. It was a recipe for disaster.

Within days I was terribly homesick. My duties were arduous and I cleaned for approximately four hours every day until my knees were swollen from kneeling and scrubbing. I had no experience with children and could not relate to their needs, but somehow I managed to survive and so did they, and as time went on I grew to love those children deeply. Perhaps their vulnerability and need for me made me feel, at last, as if I was important to someone, even though they were so young.

Being totally independent brought more confidence and I decided to try and remove myself from the memories I was hoping to leave behind. No one would ever know what had happened to me and by not telling people it would mean that I would become like them. I would become normal and it would all just go away. How it easy it sounded then, but how hard it was! How can you behave normally when you don't trust anyone? How can you enjoy your femininity when you can't allow anyone to see you that way? In 'taking charge' I unwittingly embarked on a path of self-destruction. I quickly began to binge eat and gained weight rapidly, subconsciously making myself unattractive to the opposite sex I thought. I had my hair cut very short and didn't wear the make-up you would expect a teenage girl to like. I didn't possess a skirt or a dress and lived in baggy tops and jeans. I realize now that I was trying to strip myself of my gender, hiding the shape of my body, and for one week of every month I would try not to leave the house just in case anybody knew that I was having a period – in my eyes, such things just made me disgusting.

I stayed in London for nearly a year, and then took up my place on a secretarial course based in Tonbridge. This meant moving back home again and commuting to college with my father every morning. It was difficult to settle into home life again after tasting the independence of working away. My three siblings were all away at university and so there were just the three of us, my mother, my father and me. My friends were also away pursuing their own careers and I recall feeling desperately lonely during the year of my course. I had reached a point in my life where I couldn't find my place in the world and was unsure which path to take. I knew that I wanted to travel but lacked the confidence to just buy a ticket and go. So I answered an advertisement in the national press for students to go to America for three months and work with children of all ages in a summer camp. Amazingly, I was accepted and two weeks after my 18th birthday in June 1983 I left for the States and embarked on my first big solo challenge.

Marriage and Betrayal

However long I had tried to believe that I was normal, nothing would prepare me for the realization in America that I was, in fact, still desperately scarred from my abuse seven years before. I found myself surrounded by males of all ages all living, sleeping and eating within the same compound as myself. I felt enormous pressure to be flirtatious, to go out on dates and to be similar to the other girls working alongside me. Many of them were already involved in sexual relationships with their partners and I recall feeling quite sick at the thought that if I wanted to be like them it would mean I had to become sexual myself. Never in my life had I ever wanted to become sexually active, the word itself conjured up vile and disgusting images to me, images that had been created in my head every time my abuser had satisfied himself at the expense of my childhood innocence. So, I kept away from danger and chose not to become seriously involved with any of the young men who seemed fascinated by this shy English girl who kept blushing and never wore any less than two layers of clothing.

My time in America was, despite my romantic denial, one of the best times in my life. I enjoyed the freedom of being independent, the excitement of being in a foreign country and, by being surrounded by people who didn't know of my past, I could create this person who appeared confident. I found that I could make people laugh and by doing so I would then be accepted as a person whom others wished to be around, and I revelled in my newfound status as someone 'cool'. It was a carefree time for me that, unfortunately, ended all too soon. In September I flew home and as I landed at Gatwick Airport, the familiar heaviness returned and I knew that my reprieve from reality was over.

The next challenge for me was to find myself a job. Luckily, a good friend from college had already secured a job working in West Sussex and there was a secretarial vacancy at her company. I went for an interview and was offered the position. I was on the move again, as the job was over an hour's drive away from my parents' home and it seemed more sensible to move in with my friend until I could find a place to rent. So once again, and for the last time, I left home.

My life settled down dramatically once I started work. The familiar routine of going to the office during the day and then perhaps going out with friends in the evening enabled me to feel part of normal life. Outwardly I behaved like a normal 18-year-old; I drank too much occasionally, smoked much too much and allowed myself to enjoy the club scene and the romantic interludes. And yet still I could not allow myself to participate in a physical relationship. I would allow a romance to last as long as possible before the pressure grew to make it sexual and then I would end the relationship, often with no explanation, and go back to being single. This pattern continued for a long time, constantly denying my abuse but still suffering every single day from the effects of it. Of course, I did eventually consent to sexual relationships, but because I knew I would have to one day anyway, it was a calculated acceptance that I would have to do it or I would never be 'normal'. It just reminded me that men have the right to control women, my abuser had made that clear to me when he took my body without asking, so therefore it was expected of me to have sex, and it would never be an option to say no.

The next few years passed so quickly. At 21 years old I met and married my first husband and in 1989 my son was born. To be married so young was possibly an attempt by me to remove myself from the relationship scene and my husband was a kind, considerate man who ultimately deserved more than I could ever give him. I had very little to do with the arrangements for my wedding – as I had done all my life I allowed my parents to decided on what was best for me. I thought that because they were paying for my wedding then it meant they could make decisions regarding the whole event. The guest list was made up of their friends and very few of mine, in fact there were many names on the list that I had never heard of but still I didn't think to argue! I am amazed now to think of how submissive I was then.

The day of the wedding arrived and my father and I arrived at the church. On the vicar's signal, the church doors were thrown open and I began to make my way down the aisle. It was then that I realized that staring right at me with the familiar smirk on his face was my headmaster. My parents had taken it upon themselves to invite the man who had abused me day after day, month after month, to my wedding. The one day that I should have had no worries was suddenly turned upside down and I recall stumbling as I tried desperately to maintain some composure. Realizing that there was nothing I could do, I carried on and the service continued but as I knelt at the altar I knew that somewhere behind me, my past was staring at my back. I felt such rage that he should be there, rage and hurt directed both at him and at my parents for assuming that I wouldn't have any objection to his presence.

After the ceremony we returned to our house for a reception in the garden. Following tradition we lined up to greet our guests and I waited with sick feeling in my stomach. I knew that sooner or later my abuser would appear and I was unsure of how to react. Instinct told me that I couldn't make a scene, it was neither the time or the place but I was unprepared for his arrogance. As he drew level with me, he leant forward and went to kiss me on the cheek, all the while with the familiar smirk on his face. I pulled back quickly and his attempted kiss went wide and I had the satisfaction of seeing a look of embarrassment and anger on his face. He was then forced to move on as there were other guests queuing behind him and I breathed a sigh of relief. Hopefully now I would be able to avoid him for the duration of the reception. However, sometime later, after the formalities of the speeches, I was relaxing in the company of some of my work colleagues, being teased about whether or not I was wearing a garter and if I was, being encouraged to show the girls. I dutifully obliged and lifted my wedding dress above the knee, as I turned round to show them I realized that my headmaster had suddenly appeared beside me and was touching me on the thigh. He whispered in my ear about how much he would like to see my garter for himself. I felt as if I had been struck by a thousand volts of lightning and immediately dropped my dress. I remember telling him where he could go and then I fled, shaking and close to tears. Unbeknown to me, my sister had seen me run and followed me out of the marquee. When she caught up with me I told her what had happened and her eyes blazed with anger. To my horror she turned on her heel and went back inside, making straight for him. I knew I had to stop her, even though I secretly wanted to see her attack him, so I ran after her and managed to hold her back, telling her that he wasn't worth it. Other guests had noticed the fracas and I was anxious not to turn my wedding reception into a brawl, so apart from calling him names that I prefer not to document, under her breath but loud enough for him to hear, my sister reluctantly moved away and we tried to appear normal. He wisely stayed away from me for the rest of the day and I gained a measure of satisfaction from his obvious discomfort.

Sadly, but not surprisingly, the marriage didn't work and after four years I found myself single again but this time with a very young baby to look after. I accept now that relationships do fail, but I also know that when one person in a partnership is not being honest with themself, it is only a matter of time before cracks become too wide to overcome and the relationship will end. My low self-esteem and my belief that anything physical or sexual was wrong and dirty became barriers that were impossible for anyone to live with and although I desperately didn't want to be that way, I seemed powerless to change my thought pattern. It had been with me for so many years. If I'm honest, I would say that because I didn't know how to be any other way, I was also scared of changing it, because that would mean I would have to go back in time and face the demon that was my childhood abuse.

Having left my marriage, I struggled to survive on my own. My marital home had been repossessed two weeks before the Chrismas of 1991 and I was placed, with my son, in a council bed and breakfast hostel. However rough it may sound, and indeed at times it was a desperate place to be, there were also times when I had never felt happier. We may only have had one tiny room to live in but my baby son and I had each other and we had a roof over our heads. He was, and still is, my pride and joy and even now when I look at him almost a teenager, I can remember the bond that we developed and how everything we did, we did together. Unconditional love – it was the very first time I had ever experienced it and I loved it. I was relieved not to be in a relationship and although, when my son was in bed at night, I used to feel very lonely, I was free from the expectations of being someone's partner and all that entailed.

Losing My Way

As is the way of the world, sometimes you have to reach the very bottom of the pit before you can fight your way back up again. Such is true in my case. In April of 1992, whilst my son and I were still in a hostel waiting for housing, my sister was killed in a road traffic accident. Her death devastated our entire family and I lost the person to whom I had turned as a troubled teenager. She used to fight my battles for me and despite suffering from depression herself in the last years of her life, she gave me unfailing love and support during the break-up of my marriage and my time as a single mother. I couldn't envisage life without her in it. We had never spoken in great detail about my abuse, but I knew that she felt guilty at not being able to stop it from happening and she showed me enormous love up until the day she died. To this day I miss her more than I can put into words.

Sadly, my abuse reared its ugly head once again during family discussions about the guest list for my sister's funeral. We had placed a death notice in *The Times* newspaper and my parents had been contacted by many of their former friends who very much wished to attend. One such friend was my abuser and his family. My parent's reaction caused me so much pain; in fact I still find it hard to come to terms with what happened next. They told me that they had written to my abuser telling him that under no circumstance was he to attend the funeral. The reason they gave was that my late sister absolutely hated him for what he had done to me. I struggled to come to terms with this reasoning – my parents had allowed this man to come to my first wedding, and they had not told me that he was attending, and yet they were refusing to allow him to come to the funeral because my sister hated him? This man did not abuse my sister, he abused me and yet her feelings in death had come before mine in life. They had not hesitated in almost ruining my wedding day but were quick to over-dramatize the effect he had had on my late sister. Once again I felt like a second-class citizen, and I know how angry my sister would have been if she had known. Needless to say, it was the subject of many arguments and only our grief at our loss prevented it from splitting our family apart, but I came very close to just walking away from everything and never looking back.

I began to suffer panic attacks that I knew must be grief-related. I also began to self-harm, presumably in a effort to punish myself and the world, I would use a knitting needle and drag it down my forearms over and over again until they bled, and on more than one occasion I would hit my head against a wall and then tell my friends that I had taken a nasty fall. It seemed that I wanted people to be concerned about me and when they were, I remember feeling important. Somehow this made my self-harming worth the pain. This was undoubtedly the lowest time in my life, but it also, eventually, marked a turning point for me.

As a family, we all dealt with our bereavement in very different ways, but the most obvious thing was the fact that we didn't turn to each other. We comforted each other physically of course, but we all retreated into ourselves and I realized that we didn't know how to support each other because we had never been able to discuss our feelings or fears when we were growing up. My two remaining siblings and I were more comfortable discussing our loss but none of us knew how to comfort our parents. I cannot imagine the pain they must have suffered at losing a child; being a parent myself I couldn't then and cannot now even begin to describe what they went through. All I know is that the pain I felt at losing a sister must have been nothing to the pain they felt and still feel now. What saddens me is the fact that we were unable to talk about her death in a way that might have brought us together as a family. It seemed that the gap between us was too wide to bridge, even in the most tragic of circumstances.

Having spent so long being angry, experiencing bereavement made me realize how mortal we all are and how precious life is. I knew that I must take with me the lessons that losing my sister had made me face. I felt that I owed it to her to try and make something of my life and to cut free from the past.

Love Brings Hope

In August of 1992, my local council supplied me with a home of my own and I was able to begin to create a more stable home environment for my son and myself. I made new friends that became a support network for me and I began to feel better about my situation and myself. I had the occasional relationship but was content being single and even took the step of trying therapy to help me overcome my problems. Unfortunately, the therapy didn't work for me. I wasn't ready to tell my story and therefore my counsellor was unable to help me. The quick fix I had hoped for was not to be, so we parted company and I decided that I would try to cope myself.

In 1994 I met my future husband. We shared an instant attraction and we both knew within a couple of weeks that we should be together – he provided me with much needed laughter and fun in my life and was, and still is, my rock. I told him very brief details about my abuse early on in our relationship. I wanted to warn him in a way, that I had severe emotional difficulties regarding physical contact, but with his support and understanding I felt stronger than I had ever been. We married a few months after we met and within a couple of years we had gone on to have two children of our own. However many times I tested his love for me, he never walked away from me and I began to feel that we would all be able to live happily ever after – maybe if I tried hard enough I could pretend my abuse never happened and become a 'normal' wife. I was so envious of our friends who seemed to have the 'perfect' marriage, envious of their obvious desire for each other and how comfortable they were with their physical relationship. Never in my life had I allowed myself to 'let go' and be spontaneous. I refused to allow myself to be sexual, I still believed that it was a characteristic that only men were allowed to have and I just didn't know how to give myself permission to be like other women and enjoy being myself. Luckily for me, I had a husband who believed in my ability to eventually overcome my fears and never pressured me in any way, but I was angry with myself for being, as I saw it, weak.

And so our life continued in this way, I was happy in my role as a mother to three children and devoted my time to making a home for them and my husband. I had a group of exceptionally loyal friends who supported me through the difficult times and I felt blessed to have been given the stability I had always longed for. Unfortunately, this stability was about to tested beyond any imaginable limit as we entered a period in all our lives that would change us forever.

Let Battle Commence

Over a period of a few months, I had been watching with great interest the development of a relationship one of my school friends, Sophie Rhys-Jones, was having with the Queen's youngest son, Prince Edward. The media were full of 'who is she?' 'where has she come from?' questions and it was bizarre to see such a familiar face splashed across the newspapers and television screens on an almost daily basis. Eventually, as predicted, the couple announced their engagement and in the days running up to their wedding I noticed that Channel 5 had made a documentary about Sophie's life that was due to be screened the week before the big day. My husband and I made a point of noting the date and time so that we wouldn't miss it, and on the evening in question we sat down together to watch it.

Approximately 10 minutes into the programme I came face to face with my headmaster. It had never occurred to me, naively maybe, that they would interview him for this programme. Looking back on it, of course they would, every documentary ever made about future Royal brides had always included interviews with former teachers etc., but it was a thought that had not crossed my mind. As it turned out, my husband had had reservations about the programme but was caught in a situation where if he mentioned it to me he might put into my head the thought of the headmaster appearing in the programme. He chose not to mention his concern and I probably would have done the same. Nothing could have prepared me for the horror of, once again, having to look at my abuser's face and I reacted with a violence that I didn't know I was capable of.

I remember running from the room into my kitchen and picking up cups and throwing them, anything close at hand went flying and only my husband grabbing my arms and forcing them to my sides stopped me. He then held me so tight that I could hardly breathe, but he managed to prevent me from moving and subsequently doing myself any harm. I cried and sobbed and I felt so frightened, it was if my abuser had found me after all these years and managed to infiltrate himself into my stable, happy life. He had tracked me down and had come back to start again. My conscious mind knew that he wasn't really there, only a face on a television screen, but the 12-year-old within me was terrified. The television was immediately turned off and for the next few hours, after I had calmed myself to a point, my husband and I spoke about my reaction. As we talked we both felt immense frustration at my reaction after all those years, and it seemed that whatever the answer was we had no idea where to look for it. Having attempted counselling and failed already, I could not think of any other avenue open to me to try and exorcise my past but we also knew that the time had come to put an end to the effect my abuser was obviously still having on me. The question was, what could we do? How do you pick up something that happened 25 years ago and make it go away? I didn't know the answer, but unbeknown to me, my husband lay awake hour after hour trying to find a solution to help his wife and eventually he knew what needed to be done.

A few days later I took a call from my husband from work. He told me that he had made contact with the Child Protection Unit at Crawley police station and had spoken to an officer asking for advice. He was told, quite rightly so, that the initial contact needed to be made by me as I was the person looking for their help, so we were given a contact name and the door was left open for me to make the first move. My initial reaction was one of anger and great fear. I was angry that he should have taken such a step without consulting me first, but in the same breath I understood why he had done it. In the past, any suggestion made to me regarding seeking help had been met with a firm 'no', therefore it made sense for him to gain some information before mentioning it to me. He needed to plant the seed in my head and allow me to think it over in my own time without any outside pressure, so for the next three days and nights I remember being unable to eat, sleep or think of anything else. I was sure that it would be impossible to launch an investigation into a crime that had taken place so many years before and was reluctant to get my hopes up only to have them dashed. I was terrified of having to inform my parents if I did decide to seek a prosecution against my abuser – after everything that had happened, I was still sure that their loyalty would not be aimed at me. In my eyes they had chosen to continue their friendship with the man I accused of assaulting me and had therefore chosen him over me. Any subsequent prosecution would mean they would be called as witnesses and I was absolutely sure that they would refuse.

Eventually I made my decision. Perhaps I had always known what it would be, I don't know, but one afternoon as I watched my children playing, I tried to imagine what I would do if anyone ever laid a hand on any of my precious babies. I tried to visualize my reaction and I knew that I would quite happily go to prison for the sake of my children. It was then that I knew what I had to do about my own abuse. I had to try and seek justice, not just for me but for my own family. I have never had a normal view of being female, and I was terrified that I might pass on my fears and phobias to my own two young daughters when they reached puberty. How could I possibly teach them that it is OK to be sexual and to be proud of who they are if I had never experienced it for myself? Maybe if I could find my own peace it would enable me to move on from my abuse and feel free at last, and that surely would be of benefit to my own two girls.

So the following morning, I picked up the phone and I called the Crawley Child Protection Unit. It was arranged that an officer would come to see me in a few day's time – the process had begun.

Telling My Story at Last

Before seeing the police, I realized that I had the difficult task of informing my parents of my decision to try and prosecute. I was gripped with fear at the thought of having to pick up the phone and spent hours dialling the number and then quickly replacing the handset. I was angry with myself for being so weak but deep down I knew that I was unlikely to get the response that I really wanted. It is not my intention to be judgemental of my parents but I only had my memories of what happened when I was 12 to gauge their reaction to my news. I had seen them continue their friendship with my abuser and his family and I knew that they would be unlikely to support my fight for justice, but I still hoped to be proved wrong. In the end, I was not brave enough to ring my father so I enlisted the help of my older sister. I had told her of my intentions and she had been incredibly supportive and offered to make the phone call for me, an offer I very gratefully accepted. It was agreed that she would ask my father to ring me himself after she told him my news. My stomach was in knots waiting for that call, how would he react? Would he be angry with me? But most importantly, would they understand why I needed to take this drastic action?

Alas, my worst fears were realized. My father and I spoke the next day and he made it clear, in no uncertain terms, that he and my mother didn't support what I was doing and thought that I was wrong to put the family through such an ordeal. It became clear immediately that he was frightened of recriminations from the past. Obviously, should he be called as a witness, then his behaviour after I told him about the abuse, would be called into question, the defence lawyer would demand to know why he and my mother had continued to socialize with my abuser and his family even after I had made it clear what had been happening.

Once again, but 25 years later, my feelings were less important than theirs. The pain I felt erupted as raw emotion. I sobbed until my whole body ached, unable to accept that they would not support their own child. I hadn't asked for their permission, I was telling them out of courtesy what I was about to do and yet I was accused of being selfish, in fact my father even suggested to me that I was suffering from 'false memory syndrome', in other words, I was making the whole thing up. The question now had to be, was I brave enough to take the risk of tearing my family apart and putting my own family through all the pain that would go with it? I had three young children and they were and still are my first priority, and I was scared that they would suffer. Above all I knew that should we end up in court then I would be required to take the witness stand and tell a courtroom full of strangers the full extent of my abuse. I would have to give intimate details, embarrassing enough to think about let alone tell in full detail to a jury. What if they didn't believe me, after all it would be a 12-year-old's word against his? All these things became enormous reasons for me not to speak to the police, but inside me I knew that I had no choice. Whatever my reasons, the truth of the matter was that this man had committed serious assaults on me on a daily basis and even after I left the school he had continued to be headmaster for many years – what if he had carried on doing it to other pupils? I had to try and bring him to justice, so I kept my appointment with the Child Protection Unit and a few days later they sent an officer to my house.

I have spent my life with very little contact with police officers of any kind, so I was nervous when the officer from the CPU arrived. Unnecessary nerves, as the officer concerned was the kindest, most compassionate man and I immediately felt that he was on my side. He didn't talk at me, but he talked about the procedures involved in such prosecutions in a way that I understood. He explained that after initial investigations a file would be sent to the Crown Prosecution Service who would then make the final decision as to whether there was a case to answer in a Crown Court. The most important thing I had to do would be to tell him everything that had ever happened, everything I could possibly remember, and then let them do the job of finding the evidence. And so, after 25 years, I finally had to tell a complete stranger all the intimate details – never before had I told everything, not even to my husband. I had always minimized the abuse, always finding it too difficult and too humiliating to go into every detail, but I knew I had to trust this man and I also knew that if we had any chance of punishing my abuser then I would have to be completely honest with the police.

I found myself remembering the most bizarre things, such as the colour of his shoes and the smell of the leather on the furniture. I could describe the layout of his study in the utmost detail and in remembering these things, I began to recall in extraordinary detail, separate incidents that had long been pushed to the back of my mind. It was as if someone had finally given me permission to tell the whole truth and promised me that I would not be in trouble for doing so, and as a result of the lifting of any threat my memory returned with unbelievable accuracy.

For nearly an hour, the officer gently prompted me to speak, and on the other side of the room sat my husband with tears streaming down his face. I suddenly realized how hard it must be for him to hear what I was saying – he was supposed to be the closest person to me and yet he was hearing things that I had never told him and he was overcome with guilt that he had never realized the true extent of my abuse. Of course it was not his fault, I had chosen to shut him out and in doing so I had unwittingly hurt him. For that I felt terribly guilty. By protecting myself, I had allowed the two of us to live a lie and he did not deserve it. We both knew that things would never be the same. I felt immense relief that I no longer had to live in secrecy and I trusted my husband enough to know that from now on it was not just my battle, it was ours.

When the memories finally ran out, I knew that I had to ask the officer the one question that had eluded me for all those years – did he, as someone who spent his working life investigating child abuse, think that my headmaster had done anything wrong? Even after all those years, I still harboured a secret fear that my abuser had been right about it being my fault and I had been in the wrong. His answer was what I had been praying for, he told me that in his opinion this man needed to be investigated, he said that his behaviour and actions were most definitely inappropriate and I *had* been assaulted. The relief I felt is indescribable – someone believed me and they were willing to take up the fight on my behalf.

When the officer finally left, my husband and I looked at each other and I burst into tears. Something inside me knew that I had made the right decision and however frightened we both were, we were in this together and would fight to the end. I realized that I had needed to be in my thirties to have the strength to take on such a battle. I wasn't mentally ready before and I didn't have the support required when I was in my twenties. The officer had told me that many of their 'historic' prosecutions happened when people reached the age where they had their own families and were stable in their personal lives, and it was encouraging to know that my case was not so unusual to the police after all.

Unfortunately, because the offences took place in Kent and I was now living in West Sussex, it meant that my local Child Protection Unit were unable to undertake the investigation, so the case was referred to Ashford Child Protection Unit and they sent a female officer and a senior detective to my house about two weeks after I had spoken to the original officer. I remember the day so clearly, as it was the day after my 34th birthday and my husband had taken me to the cinema the night before to take my mind off the impending police visit. I was a complete bag of nerves. So many times in the previous two weeks I had decided not to go through with it because I knew that once a formal statement had been made, it would pretty much take any decision to prosecute away from me – it would be out of my hands and there would be no going back. But I allowed the police to come and once again I embarked on a detailed description of all the incidents I could remember, this time knowing that it would end up as my formal statement. Reading it back I was confident that I had done the best I could to remember everything and the Detective Inspector who spoke to me afterwards was satisfied that they could now launch a full-scale investigation. My part, for the time being, was over and I knew that it was vital that I try and return to some sort of normality for the sake of my husband and my children. I had to remind myself that it was now up to the police to investigate and it would take time, I needed to be patient. Before they left, the officers explained that the hardest thing for them would be if they were unable to find any more victims of this man. As it stood, to go to court with just my word against my abuser would make for an unlikely scenario. The Crown Prosecution Service only refers investigations to Crown Court if they feel that there is enough evidence for a conviction and my statement alone would not warrant that. It was important that we did not become complacent – just because I had been brave enough to contact the police it did not mean that anything would come of the investigation. There were no guarantees and even though I couldn't bear to think about it, I had to accept that it might all come to nothing.

The Waiting Game

The days and weeks went by and I was surprised at how normal life managed to be. There was a definite element of relief in having unburdened myself to the police. I felt that I had been able to pass control over to someone else and now, in a way, it was their problem.

One Sunday morning, my husband went downstairs to pick up the paper from the doormat. When he returned sometime later I noticed that he was looking pale and shocked and didn't say a word to me as he passed the newspaper to me. One look at the front page and I shot out of bed with my hand to my mouth. There in big bold letters was the headline 'Sophie's former headmaster investigated for child abuse'. I just sat there saying 'oh my god, oh my god' over and over again, unable to believe that the media had found out about the investigation so early on. I didn't know what to think and was terrified that this media interest might have jeopardized our case. I was also frightened that they might find out who I was and that myself and my family would end up plastered all over the papers. What concerned me most was that my abuser would find out where I lived and would try and make contact with me – being able to hide behind the police had given me security and the thought of being vulnerable was very worrying. This concern turned out to be unfounded because the telephone rang and it was the Detective Inspector warning me about the story being broken. Apparently he had received a call from one of the Sunday papers the previous night and had been obliged to confirm that an investigation was taking place, although my anonymity was guaranteed. The media were, apparently, legally obliged to protect my identity due to the ongoing investigation, and I felt reassured by him that this would not hamper our case. Having been warned to be on my guard from now on, I was satisfied that this interest in our case was harmless.

Harmless is perhaps the wrong word to use. On that Sunday morning, all across the country, fellow pupils from DCPS had read the Sunday paper that ran the story and, unbelievably, one by one over the next few days they began to telephone the investigating officers wishing to share their own experience of abuse at the hands of our headmaster. Up to 20 phone calls were received and although some of them did not require further investigation, at least 15 of them were severe enough for the police to request statements from the pupils concerned. The media had provided the police with the best helping hand imaginable and I am so grateful for that.

I knew nothing of this development at the time, and the police were anxious to follow up these new witnesses before telling me. Subsequently, when they telephoned me one afternoon and told me in simple words 'Jo, you are not the only one', I had to ask them to repeat themselves again and again. I was totally euphoric and devastated at the same time, devastated for those other pupils but euphoric because I now knew that it was no longer *me* versus him – it was *us* versus him and it gave us a much better chance of victory. I cannot begin to describe how I felt. I felt vindicated in going to the police and I finally knew, after all those years, that he *was* wrong to do what he did and we were the victims, not just naughty children as we had been told. All those years at school wondering why I had been singled out and all the time thinking that no one in the school had any idea what I was experiencing, and all the time there were other children going through the same hell day after day, thinking that they, too, were the only ones. I wept for all of us.

When I gave my statement to the police, I had asked to be notified the minute they arrested my abuser. It was vital to me that I knew of that exact moment because it would be then that he would be forced to remember me. I had always imagined that he had not spared me a single thought since the day we last met, even though he had been in my head constantly, and it had always been my dream to appear one day and say 'remember me? I remember you and everything you ever did to me'. How I wished I could have been a fly on the wall on the September day he was arrested! I had spent weeks wondering if each day was to be the day they went to get him, jumping every time the phone rang but at the same time dreading the moment. Eventually the telephone did ring and the investigating officer said that they had my abuser downstairs and they were about to interview him. He promised me that he would call me later when they were done. So I paced up and down for hours, trying to imagine what they were talking about. Was he admitting anything? Would he manage to talk his way out of it and would the police believe him?

That evening I received the call I had been waiting anxiously for, but the news was not what I had been hoping for. My abuser had categorically denied all the allegations made against him and he denied even knowing some of the other witnesses. If I had stopped to think about it, it was obvious that he was never going to admit to any of the charges, but I suppose in my fairy tale, he would admit to everything and be punished accordingly and it would all be over. Reality is so different and it now seemed that we would be in for a long haul of gathering evidence and then presenting our case to the CPS in the hope that they would commit my abuser to trial. I tried hard not to be too discouraged, the investigating officer had assured me that they hadn't really expected him to admit to anything and I trusted their opinion, after all these men spent their working lives investigating people like my abuser and knew how it went. So it was back to the waiting game.

Winter arrived and every so often there would be a small reference made to our case in the national newspapers. It appeared that the original interest had been maintained and it became obvious that this investigation would be carried out under the scrutiny of the media. I began to cut out the clippings and my friends and family began to refer to me as 'the 34-year-old former pupil', the only reference ever made to me in each article. It became our standing joke and I enjoyed being teased, it made the whole situation more light-hearted and I enjoyed laughing with them at my own expense. Christmas came and went, and early in January we finally heard news from the police. They had formally charged my abuser with 16 counts of indecent Assault against 11 former pupils of DCPS. This now made the investigation official in the eyes of the law and he was bailed to appear in front of a Magistrates Court with a view to referring the case to the Crown Prosecution Service. I was shocked to hear of the amount of charges against him, but the most shocking revelation was that my own elder sister was also one of the charges. I had absolutely no idea he had ever assaulted her and because we had never talked about my own assault, we subsequently never talked about what he had done to her. She had voluntarily agreed to give a statement to the police to help their investigation against the assaults on me, and during the course of her interview told the police of her own experience at the hands of my abuser. I felt so guilty for not knowing but above all I felt terribly, terribly angry. Our family should never have reached the point where such conversations were banned – if we had both known of our experiences then at least we could have comforted each other instead of suffering in silence. It seemed such a waste.

My abuser appeared twice in front of a Magistrates Court and on each occasion he pleaded not guilty to all the charges against him. Eventually all the evidence was sent to the Crown Prosecution Service who, thankfully, decided that there was sufficient evidence to commit the case to the Crown Court for trial. I was so relieved that we had overcome the first hurdle – there had always been the risk that it would be deemed unnecessary for the case to go to trial, but the police had done an excellent job gathering statements and evidence and they too were delighted with the outcome. The date was set for June 5th 2000 at Maidstone Crown Court. The battle was well and truly on.

My biggest problem now was trying to keep my nerves and emotions under control. The trial was still five months away but it became the one main focus of my life, and my stomach would flip every time I thought of what was to come. Entering the witness box was something I never expected to have to do in my lifetime and I was genuinely fearful of how I would make it through. I was still suffering from panic attacks and was frightened at the prospect of having to keep them under control enough to say what was necessary to a jury. I knew how important it was to do justice to myself and all the other brave witnesses who had willingly joined the fight. I felt a huge responsibility to those people, they had braved their own past to help me deal with mine and I was eternally grateful to them. I hoped that they too might find the peace that I had also been looking for all those years.

Realizing how anxious I was about stepping into the courtroom, my sister and I decided that it might help if we actually went to Maidstone Crown Court and had a look at the court room. Maybe seeing it would enable us to visualize where everybody would sit and where we would be required to stand, so we made an appointment with the court. The day my sister and I stepped into Court 2 we realized how serious our situation was. All the time we were talking about giving evidence at a trial it wasn't really real, and yet standing in the witness box of the empty court it suddenly became very real indeed. Both of us shook from head to toe and I sensed panic rising within me. I didn't believe that I could do it, I was convinced I couldn't do it and was at a loss as to how to get out of it. I liken it to being on a fast train that only has one stop, hurtling towards the inevitable and being powerless to get off. Words of comfort and encouragement were useless; I was absolutely terrified and knew that I would stay terrified until the trial was over.

Reality Dawns

On June 4th 2000, the day before the trial was due to start, I sat in the garden in the sun and reflected on how we had come to be 24 hours from going to court. It felt like a rollercoaster of emotions, some highs but many lows – times of dismay at what I had got myself into and then determination to see the whole process through to the end. I don't recall ever allowing myself to think that we wouldn't win, I could only tell myself that we would, otherwise I would have lost my nerve a long time before. Losing was not an option, but how I wished that I could move time forward and make it all be over!

June 5th 2001 dawned. I always knew it would, but I hated having to wake up that morning. My only reasoning was that it had to come in order for it to be over, and all I had ever wanted was for it to be over, so I couldn't really complain. Even though I knew that I wasn't required to be in court that day, it marked the beginning of the end and I spent the day with my mind in the courtroom trying to imagine who would be sworn onto the jury. Would they be sympathetic, would they be aggressive? I wish I could have been there to see their faces and perhaps get an idea as to what they would think of me.

I was to be called as the first witness on the first proper day after the jury had been sworn in, so Tuesday would be my first day in the box. My husband, my closest friend and myself set off for Maidstone on a journey that would take about an hour. I don't recall being able to speak, my throat had closed up and I felt like an elastic band waiting to be released. We sat in silence until the peace was rudely interrupted by our mobile phone ringing to my dismay it was the police calling from the court. Apparently, the defence and the prosecuting lawyers were caught up in legal arguments and it would be impossible to start hearing evidence that day, in other words I was to turn round and go home and return the following morning. Imagine the scene, we had just spent an hour on the M20/26 with me hyperventilating and feeling sick, only to be turned back at the final hurdle and told to go home again – it was so unbelievable that the three of us just looked at each other and laughed, what more could we do?

Wednesday. We were asked to attend the court at 1.30 p.m. My sister was also due to give evidence that day which meant that we could all go together. I was so pleased to have her with me for support and also to be able to support her, after all, she had voluntarily contacted the police in order to help my case against him so it was the least I could do to be there for her. So we went and when we arrived we were met by the two investigating officers who led us into a side room. They informed us that the prosecution and the defence were still engaged in talks and that it was unlikely the trial would commence that day. In other words we were to return home once again with instructions to appear again the next day at 10.30 a.m. It was at this point that I really felt I couldn't take any more. I was exhausted from living on adrenaline for hours on end only to have nothing to show for it at the end of the day. I was finding it impossible to eat or sleep and was living on my reserves. It seemed too cruel to build us all up only to send us home again but there was absolutely nothing we could do about it. We had no choice but to return home again for a second time. We talked briefly on the journey about what possible reasons there could be for the continuing legal arguments and at some point someone suggested that maybe our abuser was considering changing his plea from 'not guilty' to 'guilty' but I felt it would be suicide to consider that option just in case it wasn't to be. I had to assume that the trial was to go ahead, it was the only way I could keep focused on what needed to be done, but deep down I prayed to a God that I had never really talked to before and I asked him to stop the trial before it began. I prayed he would make my abuser change his plea to guilty.

Looking back on this situation now, over a year later, I find it hard to believe that I was hoping the trial would not happen. I was so frightened at having to testify that it clouded my judgement on what would be justice and what wouldn't. As it turned out, justice was a word that did not apply. When we arrived for the third day at the court, we were ushered into a side room. There we were informed that, at the eleventh hour, our abuser had, in fact, changed his plea to guilty on some but not all of the original charges of indecent assault. His lawyers had struck a deal with the Judge and the prosecution that he would plead guilty to nine of the original 16 charges on the condition that he would be spared a custodial sentence. This information didn't register with me to begin with and I had to ask the officers to explain exactly what it meant. They explained that our case had been terminated through 'plea bargaining'. The accused and his legal team do a deal with the Crown – he says he is guilty and spares the expense of a trial, and they in turn spare him from a prison sentence. He gets to go home, technically a free man.

My initial reaction to the news was one of total relief and euphoria. All I could think about was that I would not have to go into the witness box. It didn't register at the time exactly what the outcome meant, all I knew was that it was over. I remember crying with relief in my husband's arms and in the confusion I didn't take notice of the fact that both the investigating officers did not seem to share our happiness. It was only much later that I realized how devastated they were at the outcome – they had worked night and day in the hope that another child abuser would be locked away safe from other children, and yet discussions to which they were not allowed to be party had allowed their man to go free.

After about an hour, the officers came to me and said that it had been decided that rather than defer the sentencing until a later date, the Judge had agreed to sentence our abuser that day. We were told that if we wanted to we would be allowed into the courtroom to hear the sentence passed. I knew immediately that I must be there, I needed to face this man again as a 34-year-old woman instead of a frightened 12-year-old, and if there was to be no trial then I knew that this would be my last chance to see him. I knew that however scared I was at the prospect of coming face to face with him again, if I was ever going to live without him in my head I had to look him in the eye. He had to believe that I wasn't frightened of him any more and I needed to replace the image I had of him in my head. The last time I had seen him he had been a man in his forties, now he was an old man in his sixties and I needed to be able to see him that way. A trivial thing perhaps, but so important to me.

The police waited until the courtroom was full and at the last moment we were led into the public gallery. I got the shock of my life, when I realized that it was packed with members of the press. I had had no idea that any of the media were to be at the trial and found it unnerving when I realized that they must now know who we were. But they were instantly forgotten when I looked around the court because there, in the far right-hand corner, laughing and joking with his solicitor, was my abuser. He looked up and I forced myself to stare right at him, a flicker of recognition came across his face and to me it looked as if he was shocked to see us there. Perhaps he had hoped that the whole business would be dealt with without him ever having to see any of his victims, another reason why we were determined to be there. I stared at him for what seemed like an eternity until he looked away – he did not look at me again. I knew, then, that I had found some peace in that courtroom. I had forced him to look away, which meant he was uncomfortable, a small victory after everything he had ever done to make me that way.

The Judge eventually appeared and all the charges were read out. This was the first time I had heard the details of his assaults on the other pupils and I was shocked to hear how similar they were. It appeared that there was a pattern to all his assaults and that we all suffered the same fate every time we were called to his study. It is absolutely incredible that this man managed to commit abuse on the children in his school for so long without detection, considering how many witnesses came forward with the same story, to this day I find it hard to comprehend. And as I listened in that courtroom I begin to feel such rage at the outcome. I may have been frightened of giving evidence

53

but it had taken 25 years to pluck up the courage to prosecute this man – for what? Six people sat in a room and agreed that he could plead guilty and they would promise to send him home, without reference to any of his victims, without hearing any of our testimonies. We had waited so long to tell a jury what kind of a person he was, but we had been denied our chance. Listening to the defence lawyer talk about this man made my pain well up into tears, as he spent nearly 20 minutes giving glowing character references and pointing out my abuser's achievement in the field of education, he told the courtroom and the press about the fact that this man was an advisor to the Thatcher government and was a leading OFSTED inspector, the fact that he had been given an OBE only a couple of years previously for his 'services to education', but the final insult was his suggestion that the witnesses must surely recognize that to send a man of this calibre to prison would be totally unjustified.

There were gasps of disbelief from the people around me, someone called out 'shame on you!' and the atmosphere in the courtroom became electric. People began to realize that this man was not going to prison purely because he had friends in high places and it would damage his reputation. They realized that no consideration whatsoever was being given to his actual crime or his victims, and that a conviction that should have carried a prison sentence was being reduced to a suspended sentence because of the importance of the criminal involved. He was given an 18 months suspended sentence and placed on the Sex Offenders List for 10 years. Justice was not a word that applied on that day in June. There was only one option for my family and me – we left and we went home.

Fight or Flight

There were no celebrations, just numbness. The telephone began to ring with requests for interviews about what had happened, word of the injustice of the case had spread rapidly, but I had no desire to talk to anyone and neither had any of the other witnesses, we were too shocked and it hadn't really sunk in. We needed to be left alone and allowed to take in the raw fact that we had failed. We may have got a conviction but it meant nothing if our abuser was still sitting at home. How could it have come to this?

One of my first tasks after coming home was to telephone my parents. My relationship with them had broken down during the investigation – they would both have had to testify if the trial had gone ahead and there was much bitterness and anger at my decision to bring up the past. I had realized early on that it was a subject we couldn't discuss and so it remained that way. They had decided that they would leave the country once they had given evidence and this decision had hurt me and my sister enormously as it meant they would not have been in court for any subsequent verdict. We had both hoped that bridges could have been built enough for them to be there to support us. The sad thing was that I always understood how difficult it must be for them. I know they carried enormous guilt for how they dealt with my abuse all those years ago and I had always acknowledged that things were very different then. There were no organisations such as Childline and abuse was a subject that no one ever wanted to talk about – a definite case of 'if we don't talk about it, it doesn't exist'. But all I had wanted was for them to put things right and support my decision to prosecute their former friend. Unfortunately it proved too hard for them to do and it subsequently made a huge rift in our family. I believe that they thought I was blaming them for my abuse. I wasn't, they didn't know it was happening so how could they possibly be responsible, but I needed them to make things right.

In the days that followed the sentencing of my abuser, I was at last allowed to make contact with the other witnesses. During the investigation we were not allowed to know who they were or to try and contact each other in case it jeopardized the case. The defence could have suggested to the court that we had all got our heads together and made the whole thing up, so it was paramount that we had no contact. Now, however, we were free to comfort each other and try and make some sense of what had happened. So about a week later six of us met at my house. It was an emotional meeting as we didn't all know each other, the abuse had been happening over a period of about ten years so we were all of different ages, but we were united in our experiences, and the grief and anger in my house that evening was evident. We all talked for hours. We had a desperate need to hear each other's stories and how we had been abused. It was as if we were finally able to put the pieces of the jigsaw together and try to make sense of how we came to be sitting there. Of all the conversations that flowed round the table that evening, one subject came up over and over again – were we going to accept what had happened or were we going to fight the Judge's decision and try and get the case referred to the Court of Appeal in London? I had been unaware that we had the option to do this, but others were more knowledgeable and knew that we had the right to fight for a custodial sentence. The hardest thing would be convincing the Crown Prosecution Service that there had been a miscarriage of justice – it is very rare for any sentence to be overturned and we knew that we would be taking on an enormous battle. There was never going to be any other decision than the one we made, we had all been through too much to just give up. We decided to fight.

Our first job was to enlist as many family members and friends to join us, as we needed hundreds of letters of protest to be sent to the CPS expressing outrage at our abuser's sentence. Finding support was easy, unbeknown to us people had already begun to write, including members of the public who had read about the verdict in the national press. It seemed that the majority of the country shared our outrage and were only too happy to put pen to paper. There were warning bells though. I spoke to the original officer who had come to see me and he told me that very few cases were referred back to the Court of Appeal. It would appear that the legal establishment was usually reluctant to appear critical of sentences passed in the courts. However, we were undeterred and a few weeks later I received a letter from the CPS stating that, although in their opinion the suspended sentence had been a fair one, they acknowledged the amount of letters of protest and would investigate whether or not the case should be referred back to the Court of Appeal. It was the first step and I felt positive about it, they had not refused outright so there was still hope. One other step that myself and the other witnesses had agreed on was that perhaps we should involve the media in our fight. We all knew that we owed them a great deal during the initial investigation and they had given us a tremendous amount of support, and therefore perhaps it would help our case if we agreed to do some interviews and tell our side of the story. The court and the jury had never been given the chance to hear the exact details of our abuse and so it made sense to allow the press to do it for us, so myself and another witness arranged to do an interview with the *Guardian* newspaper and it proved to be a good move. The story ran a couple of weeks later and we had a very positive response from the public. The general opinion seemed to be that we should be allowed to go to the Court of Appeal, and a few weeks later, perhaps bowing down to the media pressure, the CPS agreed to refer our case. A date was set for October 16th 2000, and this time I was sure we would win and our abuser would be sent to prison.

In early July a producer working for Channel 5 contacted me. They had apparently been following our case with interest, presumably because they had made the original documentary about the future Countess of Wessex, which had subsequently led to my contacting the police. They were interested in making a further documentary about the outcome of the trial and were hoping I would agree to participate. It was a difficult decision to make, not all the other witnesses were keen to take part and I was aware that there were more than just my feelings at stake. However, I was keen to have the programme made. I felt that it would be beneficial to us to keep the whole issue of child abuse as high-profile as possible. We were desperate for changes to be made within our legal system and I felt that a documentary could not possibly harm our chances.

So I agreed to be involved and so too did a handful of other witnesses, including a former teacher from the school who was delighted to finally get her chance to speak out.

It was arranged that a camera crew and a producer would come and interview me on August 1st. Unfortunately, my family and I moved house just three days before and were in a complete state of chaos when the crew arrived, but luckily it was a beautifully hot day and we were therefore able to restrict the filming to the garden. I had absolutely no desire for the interior of my home to be caught on camera – a girl does have a reputation to uphold! Anyway, the filming went well, although I was extremely nervous and I was confident that I had told my story to the best of my ability. The great news was that Esther Rantzen from Childline had been approached by the producer and had agreed to be interviewed, with me, a few weeks later and the interview was to be included in the documentary. I was delighted that such an organization as Childline would appear, it gave credibility to the whole issue and having their support was a great boost to all of us.

The rest of the summer months seemed to drag. My interview with Ms Rantzen was filmed in late August at her home and she and her husband Desmond Wilcox made the crew and myself so welcome. I was struck by her knowledge of the whole issue of child abuse and touched by the personal support she gave me. It was with great sadness that I learned of her husband's death just a few weeks later. He had welcomed us into his home and made tea for all of us. It was obvious how devoted they were to each other and his death must have come as a great shock to his family.

For us, October 16th was the only date any of us were interested in and it couldn't come quickly enough. Four months had passed since the trial and we were anxious to get on with the job in hand. The official line was that we had been granted leave to appeal on the grounds of our abuser receiving 'an unduly lenient sentence', and we were hoping that the suspended sentence would be overturned and replaced with a custodial one. Simple, I thought.

Misplaced Trust

The day of the hearing came and my husband, along with a close friend and myself arrived at the Court of Appeal for the 10.00 a.m. hearing. I remember how calm I felt that day, perhaps it was the knowledge that I was not required to take any part in the proceedings, indeed I had been told that there was no need for me even to attend, a suggestion that I instantly dismissed – there was no question that I would not attend court that day. I was also relieved to have been told that our abuser would not be expected to attend, apparently should his sentence be overturned for a custodial one, he would be collected from his home by the police within 24 hours and taken to prison. I was therefore relaxed to know that I wouldn't have to face him again, I couldn't visualize him attending if he didn't need to.

As we approached the entrance I was astounded to see photographers and camera crews setting up and I remember remarking to my husband 'I wonder what else is going on here today?'. My answer came when we entered Court 5 and were faced with rows of journalists, eager for interviews and looking for a good story. Luckily for me they were kind and considerate enough to leave me alone on the understanding that we would give some sort of statement afterwards. All I could hear was the sound of my own heart pounding in my ears, my empty stomach was churning and I was unprepared for how nervous I suddenly became. We took our seats and then, to my horror, a door on the left opened and in walked my abuser with his solicitor. I couldn't believe that he had voluntarily chosen to come to the hearing and I was immediately thrown into a state of panic. My only consolation was that he never attempted to look at any of us, and I detected a certain amount of tension within his entourage that gave me some relief. At least he appeared to be as nervous as we were and that was something. Unfortunately he was seated directly in front of me and I found myself staring at the back of his head, with my husband sitting on his hands so as not to put them round this man's throat – it would have been amusing if it hadn't been so intimidating to be that close to him again. I had not been prepared to see him again and I was angry with myself for letting myself down. With every ounce of strength I decided that he would not intimidate me and I refused to look at him again.

For the next two hours we listened to the legal arguments. Most of the words meant nothing as they were littered with legal references to previous cases and I began to wonder what on earth they were talking about. Surely it must be easy to change a sentence? Eventually we were given a reprieve in the form of a break for lunch and we gratefully left the courtroom. I remember asking one of the journalists if he had any idea how it was going, and he replied that he felt concerned about the amount of debating going on. He, apparently, had covered many stories at the Court of Appeal and seemed to know how things worked, but he urged me not to become too despondent and I tried hard to heed his advice.

The hearing dutifully resumed and once again we sat down to listen. This time it was the defence lawyer's turn to take centre stage and about half an hour into the session, I heard something which made the hairs on the back of my neck stand up and I felt the anger boiling inside me. He was an arrogant pompous man who had shown nothing but contempt for me and the other witnesses, and he began to give flowery reasons to the judge, why he should not overturn the sentence. He stated that at some point during the investigation the majority of the witnesses had expressed a desire to the police that our abuser should *not* be sent to prison. Apparently, we were all so concerned about his reputation and his family that we really didn't want him to suffer the indignity of a custodial sentence. The gasp in the courtroom was audible, probably because most of it came from me. A couple of people shouted out and were immediately told to be quiet or face being in contempt. I sat motionless, telling myself that it would still be OK and it was just lawyers fighting each other, but I was very frightened – there was a chance we would not win and I had only just realized. If the defence could make up such an appalling lie about us then where would he stop? At no point during the investigation had any of the witnesses said to the police that they did not want a custodial sentence, it was a preposterous suggestion to make – if we hadn't wanted him to go to prison then why did we prosecute him in the first place? We had all openly acknowledged our fear of giving evidence but we had never suggested that we would settle for anything less than a prison sentence.

Finally, the three judges stood up and retired to their chambers to reach their decision. We were not allowed to leave the courtroom and so we sat. I tried to speak but the words wouldn't come, the amount of adrenaline pumping through my body was making me feel dizzy and I was unable to look anywhere but at my hands. This was it, any minute now they would return and end this case one way or another. I almost wished they would never come back. But return they did, after about 20 minutes and within about ten minutes of legal jargon I knew we had lost. I could sense it in their mannerisms, I could hear it in their words. They told the court that they were unable to overturn the sentence because it had been agreed by the prosecution and defence lawyers which ultimately meant that the Crown Prosecution Service had authorized the sentence. So all this time the CPS had agreed to refer our case to appeal, they knew that we would be unsuccessful because they had agreed the sentence in the first place – plea bargaining, as it is called, had stripped us of any chance of justice.

It was at this point that I finally lost control and broke down. For 18 months I had had to believe that he would be punished for what he had done, if I didn't believe that then it would have been useless to go on. I had put my faith in the law and I had believed it wouldn't fail me. The Court of Appeal was my last hope. I knew that whatever decision was made on that day was the end of the road as far as our fight was concerned, should we fail then there were no more legal avenues open to us. And fail we did. I had to accept that it was over and there was nothing else for all of us to do but try and put it behind us and carry on. How on earth do you do that? I felt so angry and betrayed by the system to which I had turned for help, I didn't feel that the fight had been worth anything and more importantly, I felt that my abuser had won and that he had once again triumphed over us. He was a free man, a convicted sex offender, but still a free man.

When the decision was given by the judge, there were

cries of 'shame!' from the public gallery, the place erupted and many people leapt to their feet. My husband let his composure slip for a second and shouted to my abuser 'have you any idea what you have done to these people?'. Other, unprintable, things were aimed at the judge and for a while it became quite tense and aggressive. My abuser looked visibly shaken as he was hurried out of the court-room escorted by two security guards – what a laugh to have him escorted because he feared for his own safety, he never ever cared about ours. The courtroom emptied rapidly with the members of the press eager to get their interviews. I however could not move, I sat sobbing with my husband helpless and trying to get me to my feet, wanting so much to help me but knowing that there was nothing he could do or say that would take away the pain. I just wanted a moment to myself, I knew how many journalists were waiting but I didn't want to talk to any of them, I wanted to go home. Eventually, I managed to slip out unnoticed and made it to the ladies' cloakroom; the face looking back at me in the mirror shocked me. I was ashen and red-eyed, I looked defeated and I didn't know what to feel, but as I tried to patch up my hair and straighten my clothes I had a surge of anger, why was I cowering in the ladies' loo? I had done nothing wrong, I needed to smarten up, put on the lipstick and go out with my head held high. No more being the victim – we lost but we were not losers. So that's what I did.

The next hour or two were actually quite surreal. Here I was, a normal mother of three leading a pretty normal life, and yet when my husband and I stepped out of the Court of Appeal a barrage of television cameras, lights and journalists met us with microphones thrust into our faces. It would seem that we had made the headlines and they wanted a response. Myself and the other witnesses struggled to give as many interviews as we could, trying desperately not to look like rabbits caught in car headlights, although we must have looked as bemused and terrified as we felt. We knew that the injustice of what we had suffered that day needed to be told, and it was important that we told it from our point of view. When, at last, there were no more journalists asking for statements, myself and the other witnesses who were there retired to the pub across the road from the Court of Appeal. We sat around a large table and for about five minutes no one spoke. We just looked at each other, trying to find the words of comfort that we all so desperately needed, but unable to find any. Our respective partners looked at us helplessly; there was nothing they could say to any of us that would make the pain of the last few hours go away, so sensibly they didn't try. For a couple of hours we sat together, almost putting off going our separate ways, as if we just needed to be together, but eventually time forced all of us to head for our relevant train stations and make our way home. My husband and I caught our train at Victoria and as I sat staring out into the darkness I noticed that a fellow passenger across the aisle was reading the *Metro*, a daily evening paper available in London. I suddenly realized that I was staring at a picture of myself on the front page. Our story had made the evening editions and I realized just how much interest there had been in us that day. None of us had been aware of anything other than our task and hadn't really appreciated how important a change of sentence would have been to other cases such as ours. The message that the judges had given to the public that day was really that the legal system will always look after its own, and should a defendant be someone of high public status with friends in 'high places' then it is always going to be unlikely that they will overturn any sentence. To have overturned the sentence that day would have meant publicly acknowledging that the judge in the original trial at Maidstone had made an error of judgement, and I came to realize that the law does not like to admit that one of its own has made a mistake – it is easier for them to support the original outcome.

The Crossroads

Understandably, there were periods of great anger after our appeal failed. I know that I was very difficult to live with for a good few weeks, but I was struggling to come to terms with what had happened. Prosecuting my abuser was supposed to have given me the opportunity to move on, but I seemed unable to. We were supposed to receive justice as a reward for all the pain we had suffered over the years but we had nothing to show for what we had been through and it was hard to shut the door on the whole issue. The one thing we underestimated though was the public outcry at our failure, and for quite some time afterwards there were regular articles appearing in the national press, debating the whole issue of the sentencing of paedophiles why our legal system seemed to be failing the victims. It would appear that the guidelines sentencing across the country had not been reviewed or updated for decades. The legal system was convicting paedophiles in a modern-day courtroom but sentencing them from a pre-war guide book. We realized that we must try and get the issue looked at by the government and get them to change the laws. It would be too late for our case but maybe we could help abuse victims in the future to get justice.

The Channel 5 documentary about us had been aired a few days after our Court of Appeal hearing, and I was delighted to learn that over a million people watched it. Not massive ratings for normal weekly programmes but to me it meant that a million people now knew about the failings of our legal system. I received dozens of letters of support and outrage from members of the public and began to realize that all over the country there were people just like myself who had suffered the same kind of abuse but had been unable to do anything about it. It would appear that this was an issue that people cared passionately about and it made me realize that we must keep as high a profile as we could so that the issue did not just go away. So the letter writing began again, this time to the relevant government offices and the Lord Chancellor. We enlisted the help of our Members of Parliament to speak on our behalf and arranged numerous meetings to discuss how we would go about getting our outdated sentencing laws changed to favour the victims rather than the accused. And finally, after weeks of persistent pressure we heard the news that we had hoped for. The Law Society had agreed that plea-bargaining would be outlawed except in exceptional circumstances. This meant that unless the defendant was in extreme ill-health or they were facing a murder or manslaughter charge, the lawyers involved in their case would not be allowed to strike a deal to prevent them from going to prison. What happened in our case would never be allowed to happen again, and no one will ever have to go through what we did in order to get justice. A fantastic result and we were delighted. My delight was enhanced even more when I received a call from a journalist from the BBC telling me that Buckingham Palace had decided to strip our abuser of his OBE. The main thing his reputation had been based on was finally going to be removed and along with it, hopefully, his influence in society.

It was at this point that I began to realize that maybe you have to fail in order for people to sit up and take notice. Maybe failure for some will mean success for others and if that is the case then our prosecution was not in vain. It has been an incredible learning curve for me and all the other witnesses in our case, and we are proud of our achievements. We forced the legal system to take a good hard look at their prehistoric rules and regulations and made them realize that it was time for them to move into the new millennium. As far as I was concerned, there were no more avenues left to take and I had to accept that we did the best we could and try and move on. However, I had underestimated the determination of the other witnesses and whilst I was at home, licking my wounds and feeling sorry for myself, they were launching the next stage in what has undoubtedly become an unbelievable success story.

United Children

Looking back over the last 25 years, I feel deeply saddened when I see the catalogue of mistakes that were made. Mistakes that ultimately led to enormous psychological damage. We have come to realize, having gained more inside information during the investigation, that there had been at least two complaints by parents to the Board of Governors before and during the period in which I was abused. These parents were concerned at our headmaster's method of 'corporal punishment' and had voiced their concerns both verbally and in formal letters to the relevant departments. I had also been convinced that some of the teaching staff had their suspicions because of their behaviour when he used to try and remove me from class. I recall how one particular staff member would argue with him and try and prevent him taking me away, but always gave in to pressure and looked at me apologetically as I was led from the classroom. At the time, I did not really realize the significance but now I am appalled to think that they didn't do more to try and protect us – they chose not to act on their suspicions thus enabling my abuser to carry on destroying young lives. Their jobs and security were more important than the children in their care and they allowed their fear to cloud what was right and what was wrong. During the police investigation, a former Governor of the

71

school was approached and asked to co-operate, but he refused to discuss the matter and made it quite clear that he would not do so in the future. I consider this to be the answer of a group of people who have something to hide and I hope that they are duly ashamed of themselves. We needed their support back then and yet, when given the chance to redeem themselves, they once again put their backing behind their former headmaster, the man who subsequently admitted abusing his pupils.

Bearing in mind the significance of the above, I was surprised to receive a phone call last year from a well-respected solicitor, Sarah Harman, who is based in Canterbury. She had been approached by three of the witnesses who were determined that the school should stand up and accept its responsibility to its former pupils in its failure to provide the necessary pastoral care and protection. Whilst there is absolutely no suggestion that Dulwich College Prep School and its staff of today are responsible for a former headmaster's actions of 25 years ago, they are still the original establishment and must, therefore, carry the responsibilities that go with it.

Sarah explained that a request had been made to the school for a significant donation to the charity Childline, in recognition of our suffering, and they had also been asked to provide reassurances that their existing policies would ensure that no child at the school would ever be at risk again. Ms Harman and the other witnesses had, quite rightly, felt that since our abuser had admitted his abuse on us, then it was the least the school could do, to make some sort of gesture in acknowledgement. Unfortunately, they absolutely refused and viewed the request with the utmost contempt.

I was enraged that such a small request as a donation to

a worthwhile charity had been refused. The message it gave to us was simply, 'we didn't care then and we still don't care'. We were left with absolutely no choice, seven other brave witnesses and myself became a united group and we decided to sue DCPS for negligence. They failed to protect us, despite more than one complaint, and therefore provided the circumstances in which our abuser had a free rein. Once again, we took up the challenge and launched yet another legal battle, and once again my family and friends gritted their teeth and prepared to support me.

The first problem we encountered was the discovery that no one in legal history had ever successfully sued an establishment in such a way. Proving that a school was negligent had never been done before, there were no previous cases to refer to and no precedent had ever been set, so we were, quite literally, sailing into uncharted territory. Luckily for us, we had a solicitor who is passionate about miscarriages of justice and who had followed our original case. She seemed completely undeterred by the lack of previous cases and made a promise to us that she would do everything and anything to help us to win. We trusted her completely and instructed her to fight on our behalf for as long as it took to gain the acknowledgement from the school that they had failed us all those years ago. I can say, with my hand on my heart, that not one of us went into this legal action with the intention of gaining vast amounts of compensation. We were obviously aware that technically that is what 'suing' is all about, but our motives had nothing to do with financial gain, we needed an apology so that we could all move on.

The group consisted of eight of us, six women and two men, all of whom had been amongst the original witnesses at the prosecution. Some of us had the satisfaction of knowing that our abuser had pleaded guilty to the charges against us, but some had also had to live with the knowledge that he had not pleaded guilty to theirs. These people, even more so than myself, needed to know that their suffering had been acknowledged, they had had to re-live their experiences to the police but had come away with the knowledge that our abuser had denied ever touching them, thus preventing them from gaining any personal closure at all. I felt quite humble when I realised how fortunate I was to have at least heard him admit to his assaults on me.

It is widely known that the legal process is a long and, sometimes, frustrating one. There were weeks of inactivity when we began to think nothing was happening and then there would be a flurry of letters and e-mails and the postman would appear with armfuls of documents to be signed and returned. I am not in the slightest legally minded and I admit to being somewhat alarmed at the terminology being thrown at me, but I read and re-read every document and eventually began to understand the separate processes that come with taking a case to the High Court.

There is a fine line, apparently, between negligence and ignorance, and we had to prove that the school had had adequate warnings about the headmaster's behaviour but chose to ignore them. The school, on the other hand, was taking the stance that how could they possibly have known what our abuser was doing, therefore how could we suggest that they were negligent? We had to prove that there was enough evidence at the time to suggest inappropriate behaviour and yet it went unchallenged and ignored. We had two very strong pieces of evidence in our favour: first, there were two definite documented complaints to the school between 1976 and 1978, one of which was actually passed on to the police but no further action was taken, and second, we had a written statement from a former teacher at the school who had, herself, made a complaint regarding an incident involving her own daughter. Both these pieces of evidence suggested quite clearly that the Board of Governors must have been aware of the concerns about the headmaster's behaviour and yet no action was taken. Although I was aware of the strength of our case, it became apparent that when it comes to the law and taking legal action against a third party, you cannot be complacent. There are so many 'legal technicalities' that can make an important piece of evidence completely unusable, and even the manner in which documents are worded can mean the difference between success and failure. I could not allow myself to feel too positive about the outcome, it made more sense to look on the negative side and thus be prepared for failure. We had been convinced that our abuser would go to prison and had been proved devastatingly wrong, therefore no assumptions were made as to whether our fight against DCPS would be any different.

In November 2001 the group met in London. It was the first time that we had all been in the same room at the same time and it proved to be a difficult and emotional meeting. None of us really knew Sarah Harman and she, likewise, did not know us, so it was vital that we laid some sort of basis for our future relationship. The one vital thing that we all knew, was that we all had to trust each other. Each of us there that day had a different story and experience to tell, but our ultimate target was the same – we were there as a united group to prove how badly we had been let down by the school. Some were reserved, some more forthcoming, and it became fairly clear that no one really wanted to elaborate on the intimate details of their own abuse and, in actual fact, it wasn't necessary to do so. We all knew from the police reports that we had had similar experiences and from a personal point of view, I welcomed not having to go over the same details. It was enough to know that we understood each other and what we had been through, the rest we left up to Sarah who explained exactly what it was we had let ourselves in for.

Legal battles appear to go through stages. You are given a certain amount of time to file certain things with the court, and then subsequent time limits for further evidence to be offered to the opposition. I seemed to live my life in three-month stages, waiting for a deadline to pass and then looking ahead to the next one. I can say it became quite bizarre to be wishing away time almost to the point of missing the passing seasons and I regret doing so, I missed out on a lot of simple things because I wanted time to move more quickly than it was. But, on reflection I realized that the sooner the whole process came to an end, the quicker myself and my family and the other seven and their families would be able to finally bring the whole case to an end and put it behind us. So, just as we had done two years before, we waited patiently albeit with frustration.

Not long after our original meeting in London, our solicitor, Sarah, suggested that all of us attend individual appointments with a psychiatrist on the basis of assessing the long-term damage caused by our abuse. Rather than be put out at such a suggestion, I was more than happy to oblige. I knew that I had absolutely nothing to hide and also knew to what extent my abuse had affected me as a child and as an adult, I welcomed the opportunity to express my anger and have it documented for the 'other side' to see, at least that would mean they would perhaps understand our need for justice from them. I went up to London in December 2001 to a Harley Street clinic and was assessed by a very well respected psychiatrist who specializes in the kind of trauma that we had all experienced. He was an exceptionally kind and sympathetic man but I underestimated just how difficult it would be for me to sit alone with a man that I had never set eyes on before. The scenario of walking into his office, and sitting in front of him brought back memories of the headmaster's office that I had pushed to one side, and I found myself very emotional and more than a little bit scared. The child in me was immediately on high alert and it was only the reassurance from him that he understood how difficult it must be for me that enabled me to sit there for the necessary amount of time without running to the door. I unconsciously pushed my chair as far away from his as possible and, to his credit, he respected my obvious discomfort and did not invade the space I had put around me. All this aside, I was satisfied that answering his questions gave him an insight into the problems that I have faced all my life because of my abuse, and I came away feeling that I could not have said or done anything more.

Taking a Chance

Some time into the New Year, with e-mails and telephone calls flying all over the place, the word 'mediation' was mentioned by Sarah to the group. As she explained, it provided one last chance for the legal action to be resolved before going to the High Court, but was a complicated and highly sensitive issue that she hoped we would think seriously about before making up our minds. Mediation involves all parties concerned meeting up on neutral territory and putting all their cards on the table. An elected mediator then moves from one party to the next trying to help both sides reach an amicable agreement that would put an immediate end to all further legal action. The idea is that the two sides actually sit in separate rooms and some poor, energetic person spends hours and hours running up and down corridors passing messages from one group to the other – bizarre but apparently highly effective!

I was immediately keen to discuss the mediation idea further, as were the other members of the group. We all knew that if we continued to fight through the courts then we would be likely to have to wait a further one to two years before we would actually get to court, and although we would have willingly done so, the prospect of being able to resolve the matter in just a few weeks was highly appealing, as long as we achieved the outcome that we hoped for. It became clear that the school's insurers were also keen to go to mediation, presumably for the same reasons as ours, and so a date was agreed and set for July 2002.

As I am writing this book, looking back over the last three years of my life, it appears that each stage of the original prosecution and subsequent legal action against the school has been undertaken with precision and bold 'stiff upper lip' emotions. I can say that the reality was the absolute opposite. I became a shadow of myself during both experiences and made the mistake of locking things deep inside and trying to carry on as normal, in front of both my family and my dear friends who know me so well. It was certainly not that I didn't trust any of them to understand how I was feeling, it just became easier not to talk too much about things that I couldn't control. In the case of the original prosecution, I was only really important when I was required to make a statement, after that the legal wheels ground on without me and I received very little information at each stage. It was very frustrating and I admit to feeling angry at having to dig for any new developments myself. With regard to the legal action against the school, all the original evidence from the police was used and other than signing the necessary documents, the main body of work was done by Sarah Harman and her team, and our group could really only sit back and help when requested. Not at all how I imagined it, but I am eternally grateful that we had such a fantastic team working on our behalf.

It became apparent quite early on in our action against the school, that my particular case was the strongest. Not only had I made the original complaint to the police in 1999, but also there was documented, indisputable evidence that the school had received a complaint regarding the headmaster a year before my abuse came to light. This provided us with a firm foundation for our claim of negligence – if a complaint had been received and no action taken then our abuser had been allowed to carry on his abuse, unchecked and unchallenged – something quite unimaginable in today's society and, as has been proven, tragically damaging for all those children involved. It is important to note that although my case was the strongest, it was only in terms of the time involved not in terms of the actual physical abuse that occurred. All of the other seven members of the group suffered the same at the hands of our headmaster and I always felt uncomfortable at the suggestion that they were, perhaps, not as important. If it had not been for other ex-pupils coming forward to Ashford police at the time of investigation, we would not be where we are now and I hope that the general public and all those involved on the legal side fully appreciate the bravery of those who made an incredibly difficult phone call after, for some, nearly 30 years.

Journey's End

Finally, the day of mediation was upon us and extremely early on a Tuesday morning, my sister and I braved an unseasonably cold day and caught the train to London. We didn't say much at first until we realized that we had accidentally jumped on a slow train instead of a fast one, which then proceeded to stop at every single station between Crawley and London Bridge, visiting places that I never knew existed but will certainly now never forget! Subsequently, we were late for the most important meeting either of us had ever had to attend and we blew into the offices in London Wall convinced that we could be held in contempt of court or something similarly disastrous. As it turned out, this was extremely overdramatic as we sat down and realized that we were not the only ones having a nightmare journey. Half of the other group members were not there either, which was a relief I must admit.

The law states that what occurs in mediation between the parties involved must remain confidential and obviously we are all bound by such a legal requirement, therefore I am unable to document the discussions between the school and their representatives and our group and Sarah Harman. What I will say, however, is that it turned out to be not at all how I had visualized it to be – there was calmness, huge amounts of boredom and long periods of thumb twiddling. We drank endless cups of coffee and consumed large amounts of sandwiches for a total period of just less than 10 hours. It is quite surreal to be holed up in a large conference room for such a long period of time – there were only so many times I could call home to check on my family, and only so much that we could talk about amongst ourselves, but it was necessary and we knew that it was the only way to go forward.

Eventually, just after 7 p.m. both parties reached an agreement and the proceedings were finally ended. It is hard to really describe the feeling, some of us had been quite emotional during the day but when it came to the realization that it was over, I felt absolutely numb. It was one of those times when you know you are happy, but you can't feel it – you know you should be euphoric but can't express it. I have never experienced anything like it before. Maybe I had expected some sort of fanfare or drum roll to signal the end of the process, maybe it was just too civilized and polite, I'm not sure, but we all felt flat and took the only option available – we crossed the road, ordered two bottles of champagne and shared a last drink together before we all went our separate ways for the last time.

Saying goodbye was so difficult. I had shared the most incredible journey with these people and we had achieved an enormous amount together. In our pursuit of justice, we had managed to force the law on plea bargaining to be changed, and our subsequent action against the school had never been tried before. We also succeeded in proving negligence – two incredible results of which we are enormously proud. Above all, we were not intimidated by the voices that tried to silence us, and we refused to be disheartened when things were not looking positive. I am so proud of be part of the 'Group of 8' and will never forget the experience we shared together.

It is time for life to move on, financially I am more secure now than I have ever been but it is my emotional well-being that has been the winner. I have achieved everything that I set out to achieve and met some incredible characters along the way. There have been anger, rage, tears and laughter over the last three years, terrible black times but then always sunshine at the end of the day. I will never regret for one minute making the decision to prosecute my abuser. I do regret the pain it has caused many, many people but I owed it to the 12-year-old child in me to make things right for her. She suffered enormously and people had no idea, but the adult I have now become knows what she went through and I hope and pray that I have finally made things right. The child in me is no longer afraid.

Useful Contacts

NAPAC – The National Association for People Abused in
Childhood
42 Curtain Road
London
EC2A 3NH
Freephone Helpline telephone number: 0800 085 3330.

'Enough Abuse' Ltd website is www.enoughabuse.co.uk